How to Be a Guilty Parent

How to Be a Guilty Parent

by Glenn Collins

Illustrations by Gahan Wilson

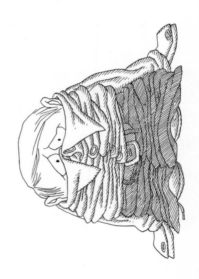

Times BOOKS

Designed by Steven Heller

Published by TIMES BOOKS, a division of
The New York Times Book Co., Inc.
Three Park Avenue, New York, N.Y. 10016

Published simultaneously in Canada by
Fitzberry & Whiteside, Ltd., Toronto

Library of Congress Catalog Card Number 82-40361
International Standard Book Number 0-8129-1034-6

Manufactured in the United States of America
83 84 85 86 87 5 4 3 2 1

FOR
SARAH, BRIAN, AND ALEX

Acknowledgments

Just a few of those who helped assuage my guilts as a parent and a writer, and who contributed to this book directly and indirectly, are: Marilyn Barnwell, Lewis Bergman, T. Berry Brazelton, David Brower, Stanley Cath, Don Colflesh, Bart Collins, John and Hind Culhane, Marion Donnelly, Delia Ephron, Hollon Farr, Stan and Shirley Fischler, Irene Freeman, Merton and Betty French, Arthur Gelb, Stephanie and David Goldman, Jody Gottfried, Annette Grant, Joan B. Harte, Steven Heller, Olga Ikaris, Eve Merriam, Jean Munzer, Nancy Newhouse, Frenchie and John Perry, Virginia E. Pomeranz, Rebecca Rikleen, Tina Robertson, Elinor Schnurr, Paul Showers, Benjamin Spock, Frank and Jo Terzuola, and Marie Winn. My gratitude to Jon Segal for making it all happen—and to Kathy Robbins for being the best.

Contents

Introduction	15
Genetic Guilt	16
Newborn Guilt	18
I. Natural-Childbirth Guilt	
II. Breast-Feeding Guilt	
III. Stay-at-Home Guilt	
IV. Can't-Stay-at-Home Guilt	
It's-Not-the-1950s Guilt	20
Gender Guilt	21
Type A: Sugar and Spice	
Type B: Puppy-Dog Tails	
Pediatrician Guilt	22
Pooh Guilt	24
Taking-'Em-to-Task Guilt	27
Reprimand Guilt	
Setting-Limits Guilt	
Read-'Em-a-Story Guilt	28
Boredom Guilt	30
Act I	
Act II	
Computer Guilt	31
Movie–Camera Guilt	32
It's-My-Turn Guilt	34
Video–Game Guilt	35
PG Guilt	36
P.T.A. Guilt	38
Culture Guilt	39
Type A	
Type B	
Baby-Sitter Guilt	40
Latchkey Guilt	41
Pet Guilt	42
Chore Guilt	43
Life-Style Guilt	44
Country-House Guilt	45

Working-Mother Guilt 46

Kitchen Guilt 47

Rich Man, Poor Man Guilt 48

We-Shoulda-Grown-Up-Poor Guilt

We-Shoulda-Grown-Up-Rich Guilt

Stepparent Guilt 49

Horse Guilt 49

Sexism Guilt 50

Moved-Them-Again Guilt 51

Sugar Guilt 52

Ethnic Guilt 54

Parent-Book Guilt 55

Gucci Guilt 55

Salamander Guilt 56

Junk-Food Guilt 58

Lunch-Box Guilt 60

Piano-Lesson Guilt 61

Birthday-Party Guilt 62

Nutrition Guilt 64

Grandparent Guilt 64

Math-and-Science Guilt 65

Train-Set Guilt 65

Exercise Guilt 67

Sunday-Night Guilt 68

On-the-Street-Where-You-Live Guilt 69

City Guilt

Suburban Guilt

Country Guilt

Peer-Group Guilt 72

Dinner-Table Conversation Guilt 74

Religion Guilt 75

Teacher Guilt 76

Single-Parent Guilt 78
Violent-Society Guilt 79
Toy Guilt 79
School Guilt 80
Public-School Guilt
Private-School Guilt
Vacation Guilt 82
Bedtime Guilt 84
Crafts Guilt 85
Meaningful-Discussion Guilt 86
Divorce Guilt 87
Visiting-Rights Guilt 88
Sleepover Guilt 90
Automobile Guilt 91
Family-Size Guilt 92
Large-Family Guilt
Only-Child Guilt

Don't-Take-'Em-to-the-
  Office-Enough Guilt 93
Hand-Me-Down Guilt 94
What-Does-Your-Daddy-Do Guilt 96
Work-a-Daddy Guilt 97
Family-Fun Guilt 97
Summer-Camp Guilt 98
College-Tracking Guilt 100
Television Guilt 101
Little-League Guilt 102
Future Guilt 104
Childless Guilt 105

How to Be a Guilty Parent

INTRODUCTION

A guilty parent? Who, me?

Yes. Me. You, too, if you've got kids and your lungs are moving in and out here in the eighties.

Is it remotely possible that any other parents in any other age have had the opportunity to feel as guilty in as many ways as we have? Did they have PG movies? Dinky Donuts Breakfast Cereal? Video games at the checkout counter?

I mean, could Ozzie and Harriet have survived the two-paycheck marriage? Could *Leave It to Beaver* have flourished in an era of joint custody?

Well, here we are, doing the best we can. This book is for guilty parents everywhere who can still manage to look themselves in the mirror and realize they're only human—and living in tricky, tricky times.

GENETIC GUILT

This is terrible. The kid *should not be born!* If she is, she'll have my *toes*, my *curly toes!* They always called me Claws at the Y camp. And she'll have my *neck click!* The strange...tiny...little...cracking sound my neck always makes in just that right weird position when I twist my head to look in the rearview mirror. And she'll need braces. A bite plate! For three years she'll be smelling up her coat pocket with the bite plate, where she hides it on the way to school! The poor kid is going to have all my dumb, lousy genes. God, she might get Grandpa's trick earlobes, the ones he could make *turn signals* with!

NEWBORN GUILT

I: NATURAL-CHILDBIRTH GUILT

"Well, actually, our doctor insisted that Gloria had to have a Caesarean, and she doesn't really remember anything at all. No, nothing.

"Well, yes, they made me leave the delivery room for the Caesarean, so I couldn't see the baby being born. No, I couldn't take pictures or do any of those things.

"But Gloria *is* going to be breast-feeding, just like everybody else."

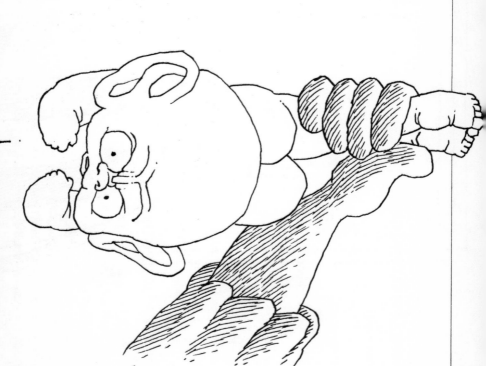

II: BREAST-FEEDING GUILT

Choose one:

(A) "Well, no, I didn't breast-feed, because it kept hurting, it made me tired, the baby was crying all the time, I had to go back to work soon anyway, and basically it just didn't work out. But of course I don't feel bad about it."

(B) "Well, yes, I kept breast-feeding so long because my husband just wouldn't help me with bottle feeding, it was so much cheaper than buying all that formula, I didn't have any job I wanted to go back to, and I didn't think it would ruin my figure. And I never imagined other mothers would say I didn't want to separate from my baby.

"But of course I don't feel bad about it."

III: STAY-AT-HOME GUILT

"Well, I don't love *every* second of staying home, Marge. But I think a mother *should* be home with her baby. No, I don't miss writing those ads and winning those awards—well, not all the time, anyway. Well, so what if Anne is getting all the good accounts now, like I would have if I'd stayed? But she hasn't had the fun of staying home all day with two small children! Well, yes, he sleeps

through the night some of the time now. And Tom helps me such a whole lot, Marge. It's just that the commute tires him out, you know? No, I wouldn't describe it as *terribly* isolated. No, never! Not more than one soap a day! Well, I try to do some reading, although last night the baby spit up all over *The White Hotel.*

"No, Marge, I just *know* I can get right back into the business any time I want! See, it's only that I like what I'm doing now so much...."

IV: CAN'T-STAY-AT-HOME GUILT

"Sure, Toni, I found a great housekeeper. The baby loves her just like she used to love me—I mean, *still* loves me—you know, when I get home from work.

"Well, Toni, I'd like to think of myself as being the living proof that a mother can do it all! That she can pick up her career only three months after her baby is born and feel just great about everything!

"Of course... well... sometimes I really *miss* her. Not being with the baby and all? I mean—you'll keep this between us, Toni?—sometimes I just want to be only a *mother.*"

IT'S-NOT-THE-1950s GUILT

My God, my kids won't have Mrs. Torregrossa in the fourth grade, like I did.

•

My kids won't grow up wearing a Hopalong Cassidy hat and a Howdy Doody shirt.

•

They won't grow up safe under President Eisenhower in a nice suburban neighborhood where there's no child abuse and no Son of Sam and no cults and no budget cuts.

•

They won't see Ed Sullivan every Sunday night.

•

They won't hear "Earth Angel" for the first time and realize their lives will never be the same again.

•

Their dream bike won't be a Schwinn Phantom balloon-tire bomber with red brake lights.

•

They won't dance the stroll in Mrs. Fitzgerald's basement to a pink record player with a 45 spindle.

•

They won't neck for the first time watching a Pat Boone movie.

•

They won't see a brand-new blue-and-buff 1957 Dodge parked on their block.

•

They won't see *Your Show of Shows* on Saturday night while they drink Coke out of a bottle.

•

Of course—now that I think about it—I really *hated* the fifties when I was a kid, you know?

GENDER GUILT

Type A: Sugar and Spice

Lordy, how will she *survive*? A tiny baby girl in a vast world of tattooed, Hell's-Angel, always-checking-out-the-centerfolds *men*! They're interested in only *one thing*—my daughter! And in the world she'll grow up in, she won't even be able to stay home and have little babies unless she first graduates Cal Tech cum laude. Otherwise, they'll make my baby girl hate herself! Oh, honey, don't hate yourself! You're just a *baby girl*.

Type B: Puppy-Dog Tails

But my son! Just a sweet, friendly, lovable little *marshmallow* in a vast world full of tattooed, Hell's-Angel, always-checking-out-the-centerfolds *men*! He will have to *prove* himself against them! And when he's a senior in high school and has his Harvard acceptance, one of the basketball cheerleaders will kidnap my son and make him marry her, and he'll have to go to work as a flange checker for the rest of his life.

Son! Don't do it! Don't! They make it so terribly hard for sons these days, my beautiful baby boy.

PEDIATRICIAN GUILT

SYMPTOMOLOGY: Immediate onset of Pediatrician Guilt can be provoked by exposing the affected parent to one of the following conversational stimuli:

•

"Oh, your pediatrician *doesn't* give you the little bottle with the green medicine he whips up to make the colic go away? Then how do you sleep at night?"

"Well, my pediatrician always spends an hour and a half with little Lisa to be sure I've asked every little thing. Doesn't yours?"

"No, my pediatrician doesn't have any telephone time. We're supposed to bring Lainie right over to the office at any hour of the day or night."

"You mean your pediatrician doesn't have Manny the Magician in the waiting room to make the kids laugh?"

"Sure, my pediatrician came over for a house call while he was on vacation last August."

•

TREATMENT: The only known treatment for this affliction is the rapid and repeated changing of pediatricians.

PROGNOSIS: Someone you know will always have a wiser, kinder, more accessible pediatrician, no matter how many you've been through. The only cure for the ailment is attainment of a child's age of majority.

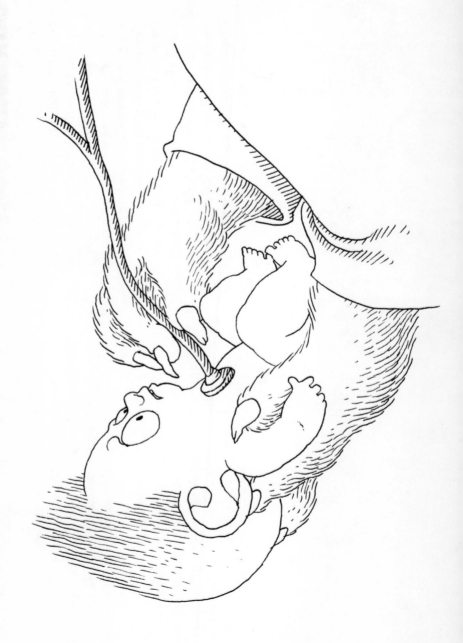

POOH GUILT

Dear Parent,

Congratulations.

You have just purchased 275 Sesame Street hand puppets, squeaky dolls, toys, pop-up books, juice cups, and assorted merchandising spin-offs.

You are now qualified to proceed with your next task.

What is your next task?

You must now expose your child to all of the Wonderful Traditional Children's Characters, without which no childhood is really a childhood.

You must complete your task within the stated time.

The stated time is from now until your child reaches thirteen years of age.

You must complete your task successfully.

If you do, you will be considered a Fine Parent who has exposed her or his children to all the Wonderful Traditional Children's Influences. You will be a success in your own eyes, in your children's eyes, and in the eyes of society.

You must not fail in your task.

If you do, other parents will make disdainful remarks. Your children, as teen-agers, will claim that you never gave them a proper childhood. And you will feel guilty for the rest of your life.

All ready to play?

Then here's your checklist. Begin playing and buying right now:

(1) All 9,000 Richard Scarry books
(2) Curious George and his friends
(3) The entire Peter Rabbit series
(4) All the Dr. Seuss books
(5) Mrs. Piggle-Wiggle and company
(6) The Mr. books
(7) Mother Goose rhymes and Grimms' fairy tales
(8) All the Pooh books
(9) Babar and his friends, relatives, playmates, and significant others
(10) *Charlotte's Web* and *Stuart Little*, in that order
(11) The Barbapapas books
(12) Raggedy Ann and Raggedy Andy books and dolls
(13) The Frances books
(14) The Berenstain Bears and friends
(15) The Strawberry Shortcake gang
(16) Maurice Sendak's books and the *Really Rosie* record
(17) The Uncle Wiggily series
(18) All 250,000 Smurf figures and etceteras
(19) *The Chronicles of Narnia*
(20) The Peanuts books, posters, pencil cases, and you-name-its
(21) The Tin-Tin books
(22) The Choose Your Own Adventure series
(23) Star Wars books, comic books, action figures, and other *tsotchkes*
(24) Superman books, dolls, toys, and comic books
(25) Super Hero comic books, dolls, and other stuff
(26) The Encyclopedia Brown books
(27) *Charlie and the Chocolate Factory* and the other Charlie books
(28) Nancy Drew and the Hardy Boys books
(29) Books and characters from all the Disney movies as they rerun them each year
(30) Barbi and Ken and the gang
(31) (Watch This Space.)

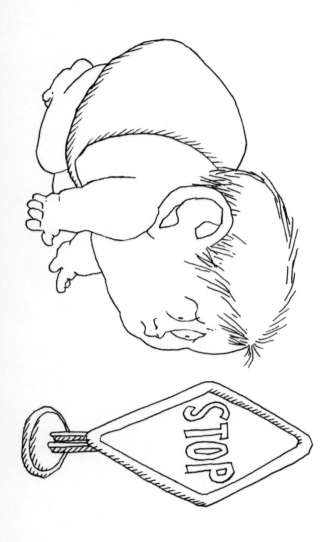

TAKING-'EM-TO-TASK GUILT

REPRIMAND GUILT

"You get to your room this instant!"

"Don't you ever do that again!"

"Stop doing that right now!"

"If I ever catch you in there again you're gonna know it!"

"Get off there right this minute!"

"Just who do you think you're talking to, anyway?"

"Cut it out, the both of you!"

"Didn't you hear what I said? That's enough!"

(Did I *have* to pop off like that?)

SETTING-LIMITS GUILT

"I just don't think a seven-year-old should be seeing Texas Hacksaw Zombies on a Saturday afternoon, that's all! And I don't care that Ronald and Jason's parents are letting them go! And, no, you won't lose all your friends."

"I don't care if you're the only one in your class who doesn't have the XR3 Kidputer! We can't afford it. And I think it rots kids' minds, anyway! I'm sure that when you're older, you'll realize that your dad was right."

"You'll get a five-speed banana bike with wheelie-grips and drag treads when I say you're good and ready! And mark my words, you'll thank me for this someday!"

(Hey, where did *you* get so high and mighty? My God, you're sounding just like a *parent!*)

READ-'EM-A-STORY GUILT

"Once upon a time there was a prince in a big castle. And he said to his father.

"And so then the prince put on his suit of armor and got upon his charger. And they headed off into the forest on the way to.

"But the Black Knight caught the arrow in his teeth and drew his sword and said.

"And so the princess looked into the prince's eyes and soon she.

"After a very long time the prince found his sword and charged at the Black Knight, saying.

"And so they all lived happily ever after."

"Skipping? Who, me? What do you mean I was skipping? Well, what, I'm supposed to read every single little line here?

"Hey, I thought you were asleep, anyway! How about closing those little eyes, huh?"

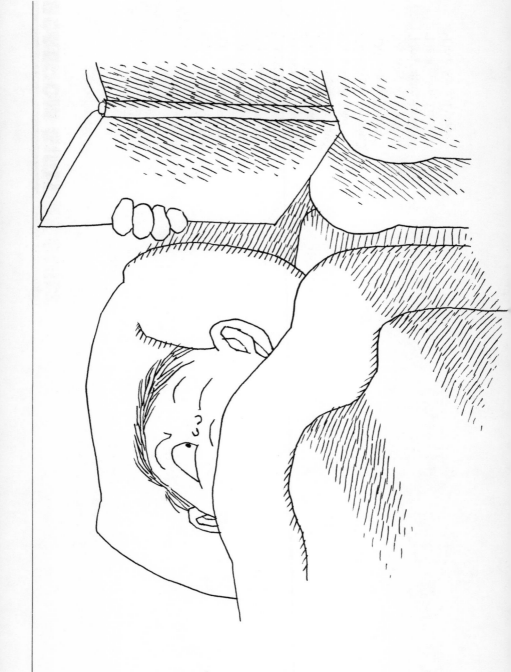

BOREDOM GUILT

Act I

"No, it's not boring, Al. I see so little of Tommy during the week that I treasure every golden moment I have with him over the weekend."

Act II

"Do it again, Daddy."
"Do it again, Daddy."
"Do it again, Daddy."
"Do it again, Daddy."
"Do it again, Daddy."
"Do it again, Daddy."
"Do it again, Daddy."
"Do it again, Daddy."
"Do it again, Daddy."
"Do it again, Daddy."
"Do it again, Daddy."
"Do it again, Daddy."
"Do it again, Daddy."
"Do it again, Daddy."
"Do it again, Daddy."
"Do it again, Daddy."
"Do it again, Daddy."
"Do it again, Daddy."

COMPUTER GUILT

WELCOME. YOU HAVE JUST ACTIVATED THE USER-FRIENDLY PARENT-AND-CHILD COMPUTER LEARNING PROGRAM OF YOUR NEW KIDDIPUTE® LEARNING SYSTEM. WE CONGRATULATE YOU ON YOUR EXCELLENT JUDGEMENT IN MAKING THIS PURCHASE.

ARE BOTH YOU AND YOUR CHILD HERE AT THE COMPUTER? TYPE IN YES OR NO.

"Yes."

DO YOU WISH TO PROCEED WITH STEP ONE? TYPE IN YES OR NO.

"Yes."

STEP ONE IS A QUESTION FOR MOM OR DAD. IS THE PARENT AT THE KEYBOARD? TYPE IN YES OR NO.

"Yes."

MOM OR DAD: HAVE YOU ALREADY PURCHASED THE $4,250 SUPERCOLOR ANIMATION MONITOR (MODEL 958Z, WITH SELENIUM-SPACKLE-FINISH CASE AND SPRING-ACTIVATED JOYSTICK) WITHOUT WHICH IT IS IMPOSSIBLE TO LEARN AND UNDERSTAND THE INTERMEDIATE PHASE OF YOUR CHILD'S ESSENTIAL LEARNING READINESS PROGRAM? TYPE IN YES OR NO.

"No."

MOM OR DAD: ARE YOU AWARE THAT UNTIL YOU HAVE PURCHASED THIS VITAL COMPONENT OF YOUR KIDDIPUTE® LEARNING SYSTEM, YOU WILL STIFLE THE DEVELOPMENT OF YOUR SON'S AND/OR DAUGHTER'S COMPUTER LITERACY? THAT YOU WILL CONDEMN HIM AND/OR HER TO A LIFETIME OF STRUGGLING FOR LOW-PAYING, UNSKILLED JOBS? AND IN YEARS TO COME, WILL YOU BE ABLE TO BEAR YOUR OWN COMPLICITY IN SENTENCING YOUR CHILDREN TO A FUTURE OF DESPAIR, USELESSNESS, AND UNNECESSARY WANT, IN A TRAGIC LIFE THAT MAY BE NASTY, BRUTISH, AND SHORT?

TYPE IN YES OR NO.

"Help."

MOVIE-CAMERA GUILT

If I don't take pictures of the kids, well, I'm just not doing my duty as every father has to do in preserving on film the important historical record of his children.

But if I'm always pointing a camera at them, dammit, then aren't I being remote from them all the time? Aren't I just some kind of an observer and not a real dad who's actually playing with them and all?

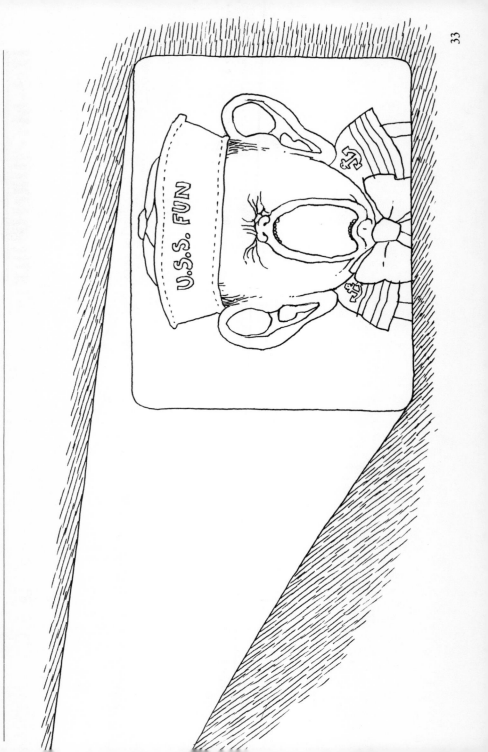

33

IT'S-MY-TURN GUILT

Dear Diary,

The baby was sick *all day* today; I finally got her to sleep at 10:30. *Just* as I began to read the new M.M. Kaye, Toni woke up again. And would you *believe* it, I found myself feeling *guilty* about reading that book? Well, finally Toni cried herself to sleep in my arms.

Dear Diary,

Tonight we finally got a baby-sitter after three weeks of Toni's colic and my depression. Well, there we were, at Howard's party, and what happens? The baby-sitter calls. Toni is throwing up. So we rush home and I'm holding Toni and she's calming down and I look at her little face and don't you know, I ask myself, "Why did I go to the damn party in the first place?"

Dear Diary,

I thought I had it all figured out this time. I left Toni with old Mrs. Schultz for a few hours so I could have a nice morning at the mall, and *of course*, when I came back, Toni was *screaming*. I said to myself, "Hey, look, don't feel guilty—it was *your turn*." And I did feel better.

And then Mrs. Schultz smiled and started baby talking to Toni: "Baby *missed* Mama. Baby wondered if Mama was coming *back*. Baby wonders if Mama *loves* her. Baby wants Mama to take her *along* when Mama goes to the mall!" And Mama wants to *sock* old Mrs. Schultz.

VIDEO-GAME GUILT

Dear Doctor Video:

Exactly how do parents afford to keep up with every new Atari, Intellivision, Colecovision, and Whatsitvision that comes along? I'm at my wit's end, Doctor Video!

OVEREXTENDED

Dear Overextended:

I'm very glad you asked me that! I think you'll feel a whole lot better about your overextension problems if you'll simply spend a few hours playing my new game cartridge, "Zap the Alien Invader Video-Game Company Exploiters," available at all fine upscale hobby stores.

Dear Doctor Video:

How do I keep my children from becoming warped, game-addicted video zombies? Doctor, it's not that I *want* them to play these games. But the kids say that they'll lose all their friends unless they develop advanced video-game skills.

CONCERNED

Dear Concerned:

How very glad I am that you asked me that! I believe the most satisfying and truly practical outlet for your concern may be a good, long session in front of the cathode ray tube

playing my new game cartridge, *"The Video-Game-Zombie Smashers," available now in fine stores.*

Dear Doctor Video:

How will my children ever learn to "love thy neighbor" when they are devouring the world while playing Pac Man and Ms. Pac Man, killing everything in sight while playing Robotron, zapping an entire city while playing Zaxxon, destroying the master programmer while playing Tron, blasting aliens while playing Space Invaders, exploding pirate ships while playing Asteroids, devastating attackers while playing Defender, blowing away enemy spikes while playing Tempest?

ANGRY

Dear Angry:

For quite some time now I have been hoping that some extraordinary reader would ask me that question. I advise you to get some of that anger out! Play a few fast rounds on two of my newly available game cartridges, "Kill Thy Neighbor With Kindness" and "Ms. Kill Thy Neighbor With Kindness." They've got great graphics and an upbeat Biblical message!

And have a nice day,
DOCTOR VIDEO

PG GUILT

"What are they doing up there, Dad?"

"Well, they're, ah, kissing, hon."

"Why is he taking her clothes off?"

"Well, see...they like each other. They like each other a lot."

"What's that thing she has on, Dad?"

"Oh...that's just her, ah, her black-lace brassiere."

"What's he doing to her now, Dad?"

"Well, he's...honey, they're making, you know, love."

"Why?"

"Well, because this is the kind of movie where they do that, and I really wanted to see this movie and I thought it'd be okay to take you along but it really isn't, and how can anyone have enough time and money to screen every movie in advance to know if you can even take your kids, anyhow?"

P.T.A. GUILT

"Hello, Mr. McAllister? I'm calling from the Parent's Association, and we were wondering why we didn't see you last night painting our giraffe murals on the lunchroom walls with the rest of us.

"Well, we know *you* work, but we were all so terribly sorry not to see Mrs. McAllister there either.

"Well, even if she works, too, it seemed to us that one of you might be willing to help us out with our giraffe murals. We'd hoped that every parent could do his or her share. There are so few of us, Mr. McAllister, and *so many* wonderful things to accomplish.

"What? Well, you can't expect a few of us to shoulder all the load while other parents reap all the benefits. I mean, Mr. McAllister, what would our school be like if every parent had that same attitude?

"No, I'm sure you don't want us to feel that you're one of those parents, Mr. McAllister. It would be a tragedy if that sort of thing got back to the teachers and the school administration or even the other children. It's awful how you never know when that sort of thing might affect your own child's positive learning experience. And that would be a terrible thing to happen, wouldn't it, Mr. McAllister?

"I'm glad you agree. Well, there are the hippopotamuses to be painted in the gymnasium tonight, and then there's the smock room swab-down-and-disinfection this weekend, Mr. McAllister. And don't forget the Quiche of the World potluck dinner next Wednesday; I believe you're Scottish? What sort of quiche do you folks make in Scotland, Mr. McAllister?"

CULTURE GUILT

Type A:

Well, I just can't believe that *we're* spending an *entire afternoon* in J.C. Penney's Tot World in this godforsaken mall, and do you know what is going on *right this very second* in the city? The Great Hall of Science is having that Mollusk Day for Kids—all afternoon! And the Light Operaters are doing *Pinafore for Preschoolers*, and the Ballet Nacional de Carramba is performing *Nutcracker*. And just what kind of stimulation are they getting *here*?

Type B:

Sure, we live *right in the city*, but have the kids ever gone to the Young People's Vermeer Lectures at the Municipal Museum Society? Oh, no, it's always television for them. I mean, for all the exposure to culture they get, you'd think we didn't even *live* in the city.

BABY-SITTER GUILT

I absolutely cannot enjoy this (dinner party, movie, stroll on the beach, tennis match, or ———) because:

The smoke alarm is playing the 1812 Overture and the baby-sitter is asleep.

•

The fuse just blew and *they're all in the dark.*

•

Grandpa will call and notify the police because a strange voice answered the phone.

•

Mother will call and the baby-sitter will insult her and Mother will come up to try to take the baby away and they'll all start shouting and wind up in jail and I'll never even know it just sitting here in *Star Wars, Part XI.*

•

The old *Parade* magazines in the hall closet will spontaneously combust.

A burglar just telephoned to case the house, and the baby-sitter has asked him to come watch TV!

•

The telephone will blow up.

•

The baby-sitter is necking with her boyfriend, and little Rickie is writing all over the walls in orange Caran d'Ache.

•

The john in the utility room just started flushing itself, and the entire basement is under water.

•

The baby-sitter put Joelie's jammie suit with the little feet on it on *backwards,* and Joelie *will completely lose all circulation in his toes!*

•

Susie will always think of me as a bad mother because I wasn't there when she woke up!

LATCHKEY GUILT

"Well, Bobby, I had the hardware store put a little plastic ring with a different color on each key, see? So you can tell them apart. Now *this* key is for the lobby door, only don't ever let anyone in you don't know. Wait outside until one of our neighbors comes along if you have to.

"Now *this* key is for the top door lock—the orange key? And *this* one is for the bottom door lock. You know that's the one that sticks and sometimes you have to push the door in and kick it and then push the door *out* and kick it and kick it and turn the key really hard to the left while kicking the door again. But that's easy to remember! I'm sure you'll have no trouble with it.

"And then if you'll just remember to keep the keys on the string around your neck, and when you're home never open the door for anyone and never answer the telephone unless it's me but *I* always ring three times first, so you'll know. Why, it'll go just *fine*, right?"

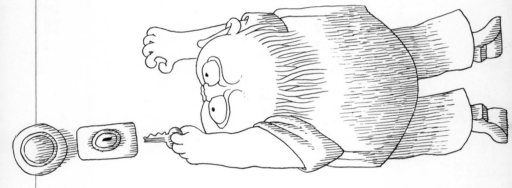

PET GUILT

"No, Mikey, your mom and me, we're both allergic to cats. Well, that means they do funny things to us. Well, we sneeze and cry, Mikey, whenever cats are around. Yes, yes, I see you're crying and there aren't any cats right here, but that's not really the same thing, Mikey. No, wait! Mikey! We *will* get you a pet. Honest! Your dad won't let you down. Well, no, dogs do the same thing to me that cats do. Okay, okay! Mikey, stop screaming! We will get you a pet, yes! Well, I did grow up with a budgie. Taught it to talk and everything, Mikey. Yes, I love them. But see, your mom...well, she hates the little scratching-zinging noise their little feet make when they claw their way up the bars of the cage, and she says she can't stand the thought of a parakeet flying around her head and landing on her hair, Mikey! No! No! Mikey! Stop crying. We'll get you a turtle, although it'd probably die in the steam heat. No, we'll get you an *ant* farm, except you know how all the ants died last time. Look, Mikey, how could your dad let you grow up without experiencing the joys of having a pet? That's your birthright. I won't let ya down, Mikey, you can count on your dad."

CHORE GUILT

"Wash the dog."

"But Mom, it's sunny out and the kids are going down to the beach."

"Wash the dog."

"But Mom, I'm just always working and I can never have any fun."

"Wash the dog."

"But *Mom*, I'll do it later!"

"Wash the dog."

"But Mom, I *never* have any fun and my allowance isn't even as much as Terry's *sister's*."

"Wash the dog."

"Okay, Mom, okay. Now you're gonna tell me about how when I was *your* age you used to have to work four hours a day in a candy store and give all the money to your *mother*, right?"

"No, that's when you ask for your allowance, hon. Right now, you're going to wash the dog, and while you do, I'm going to tell you about how when I was your age, they didn't have dogs!"

LIFE-STYLE GUILT

DEAR MOM HER IS MY CRHSMTS LIST. ALL TH
THNGS I WANT:

325 SMURF FIGGURRES
1 MERCDESE 250 SE
1 SWMMING POOL
1 LRGE ADVENT TLEVISSION SCREEN
1 BETAMAX RECRDOING MACHINE WITH
   LOSTS OF TAPES
1 $100 ADIDAS JOGINE SUIT
1 PAIR LEVIS 502 JENES
1 $320,000 SAILEBOAT
1 REDWOOD COUNRTY HOUSSE
1 SKI CODNONIMIUM

THNX YOU,
JOEY

COUNTRY-HOUSE GUILT

"So, Chrissie, you want to be back home. How? We're going to be here all weekend.

"You miss *what*? All your friends. Oh. But mostly your friend Jeannie. Your friend Jeannie's friend Pammie. Pammie's friend Buffy. Buffy's Atari cassettes. More? You miss the Sunday morning *Avenger Busters Hero Daredevil Show*? You miss the cable cartoons from Atlanta? You miss television. You miss talking on the phone to Jeannie, Pammie, and Buffy. You miss having a phone. You miss your room. You miss the kitchen. You miss the front lawn. You miss the sidewalk.

"You hate what? This house. The sun. The weeds. The lake. The boys at the lake. The girls at the lake. You hate going into town. You hate coming back from town. You hate who? Oh, Mommy and Daddy. And you'll never forgive us?

"But Chrissie, what about the swimming hole? What about catching frogs on the mountain path? What about pressing ferns in the Peterson guide? What about reading the book of the woods? What about the sizzle of steak over a wood fire? What about *my* need to flee the city? And what about the mortgage I'm paying on this place!"

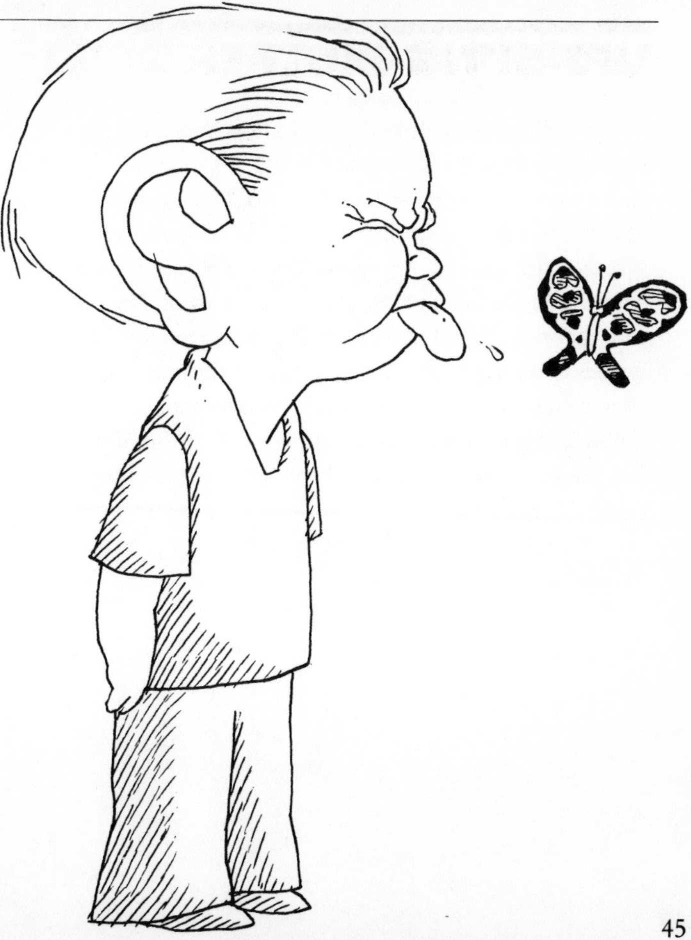

WORKING-MOTHER GUILT

"Hello, Mom? Is that you? I know you don't like me to phone you at work and all, but where's the Sweet 'n Low? Huh? Oh, it's for the *coffee*. No, I hate coffee, Mom. The coffee isn't for me. Well, it's for the firemen. No, everything's real okay now, Mom. Nothing to worry about. The firemen put out the fire right away. The fire? Oh, that was when I tried to make grilled cheese sandwiches and forgot to take the plastic off the cheese so it caught fire. I *know* that I was supposed to make peanut butter and jelly sandwiches. But I couldn't, Mom. Huh? No peanut butter, that's why. I *know* you left a whole jar in the refrigerator, but when I opened it I left it on the table and the dog ate it. The *dog*? Well, how should I know why?

"Well, Mom, I have to go give the firemen their Sweet 'n Low now, and then I'm going next door to Mrs. Jones's house. Well, when she saw the firemen come she invited me over for soda. She said she didn't believe that mothers should be working all the time to pay the mortgage and that they should stay home until their kids went away to college, just like she did. Well, bye! See you when you get home, Mom!"

KITCHEN GUILT

Oh, Dad can't cook, eh? Well, just what's the problem with this menu?

BREAKFAST: (1) Dad's Frozen Waffles with Cinnamon and Sugar on Top Because There Isn't Any Syrup in the Closet Anywhere

(2) The Bit That's Left in the Rice Crispies Box with Whatever Milk We Can Find in the Refrigerator

(3) Toast with Margarine Cut into Small Strips and Spread All Over the Plate Like There's Lots of It, with a Big Glass of Milk

LUNCH: (1) Whatever's in the Campbell's Soup Can in the Back of the Closet, with Ritz Crackers

(2) Pop's Sliced-Up Frankfurter on Whatever Bread We Have, with Plenty of Ketchup

(3) Dad's Peanut Butter Spread on Anything at All That He Can Find Around the Kitchen

DINNER: (1) Dad's Old-Fashioned Frozen Macaroni and Cheese on a Plate, While Everyone Watches TV

(2) Pop's Maybe-You'd-Like-Some-More-Cereal-Because-Breakfast-Was-a-Long-Time-Ago Dinner

(3) The Big Bag Dad Brings Home From Burger King and Leaves on the Kitchen Table

RICH MAN, POOR MAN GUILT

WE SHOULDA-GROWN-UP-POOR GUILT

Does he hang out on the streets like I did? No. Does he bump into crooks and saints on the street corner like I did? No. Does he take the crazy chances I did? No. Does he have a burning need to escape from poverty like I did? No. Does he test himself like I did? No. Does he have it too easy? Yes. The way that kid is growing up, he'll think life is a free lunch.

Well, it's all my selfishness: Am I really going to give up *this house* in *this neighborhood* for a three-room apartment in the old neighborhood? I might want to do that *for* my kids, but I could never do that *to* myself. The trouble with street corners is they have sharp edges.

WE SHOULDA-GROWN-UP-RICH GUILT

No matter how much we try, our kids are never going to have the toys, the nannies, the tutors, the tennis lessons, the ski trips, the weekend home, the summers abroad, the elite education, and the connections that the Tiptons' kids have. And they'll always blame their mom and dad. At least, until they make their first million.

STEPPARENT GUILT

She says:

"But you're not my mother! You're my stepmother and you have *no right* to tell me to get my comics off the dining room table, because you're just some stranger who walked in off the street as far as I'm concerned and I hate you and I miss my real mom!"

I say:

"Okay, I'm not your mother, but as long as I'm the adult and you're the child and you're living here, I have every right to tell you to clean up!"

I think:

No way, I am not the Wicked Stepmother, and *you*, young lady, are certainly not Cinderella, I can tell you!

HORSE GUILT

"Yes, honey. Millicent *does* have a horse, and she did braid the mane and touch it up with shoe polish and win a red ribbon at the fair. But Millicent doesn't live on West 98th Street, hon. Her neighbors are *cows*, right? Well, yes, okay, teen-age girls do have this mystical bond with man's friend the horse, but you'll just have to form your bond with a Checker cab.

"No—no, honey. No, I'm not making fun of you. *Please* stop crying. Yes, I *understand* that that's the way Elizabeth Taylor got her big acting break. But—what? What's that? Why do *you* need to butt in, Timmy? Oh, I get it. Well, *you're right*, Tim, Mickey Rooney taught that kid very important lessons about life when they trained that Arabian horse, but the closest *you'll* ever get to a black stallion is a Motoguzzi. Okay, okay! Stop crying, both of you! Please? Um, maybe we can get to a dude ranch next summer, would that be okay?"

SEXISM GUILT

Well, it sure is clear what we've got to be doing: raising our baby in a nonsexist way. It shouldn't be too hard—we're can-do parents! Let's see: We'll furnish her nursery in a nonsexist way, we'll choose a nonsexist name for her, and we'll send out nonsexist birth announcements. We'll view our developing infant in a nonsexist manner, we'll buy her nonsexist toys, we'll give her the example of our nonsexist marriage to grow up with, we'll take turns rearing the baby nonsexistly, we'll share the cooking and cleaning and financial planning so she'll have nonsexist role models to copy from, and we'll send her to a non-sexist nursery school. We'll encourage her to feel pride in her physical and emotional self in a nonsexist way, we'll help her to develop a nonsexist attitude about sports, we'll

carefully explain the sexist attitudes in every TV show and advertisement she sees, we'll correct her conversation when it reflects sexist clichés, we'll discourage her from seeing movies that portray demeaning stereotypes about women or men, we'll send her to a nonsexist grade school and encourage her to follow a nonsexist career.

And, as two nonsexist working parents who manage to find the energy to do all this in addition to advancing our own careers while somehow trying to keep our marriage from breaking up, we'll actually find the time to get our daughter's shoes and socks on before we all get out of the house in the morning!

And we'll never feel a bit guilty when we happen to *fail* doing any one of these fine things.

MOVED-THEM-AGAIN GUILT

"Mommy? Mom? Do you think there are going to be any other six-year-old girls up in Alaska?"

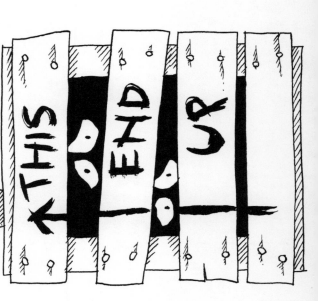

SUGAR GUILT

UNITED STATES FOOD AND DRUG ADMINISTRATION NUTRITIONAL INFORMATION LISTING

PERCENTAGE OF U.S. RECOMMENDED DAILY ALLOWANCE OF PARENTAL GUILT

(FOR RELEVANT FOODSTUFFS)

PRODUCT	% TOTAL DAILY PARENTAL GUILT
KOOL-AID TROPICAL PUNCH	4
D-ZERTA, ORANGE	7
D-ZERTA, PAPAYA	11
BUBBLE YUM, FAMILY PACK	15
SARA LEE FUDGE NUT TORTE	18
COOL WHIP	7
COUNT CHOCULA CHOCOLATE-FLAVORED FROSTED CEREAL	47
RAISINETS	4
NILLA WAFERS	3
WAFFELOS MAPLE SYRUP FLAVORED CEREAL	36
TEEM SODA, 2-LITER BOTTLE	27
DEVIL DOG, INDIVIDUAL	18
FLEER DOUBLE BUBBLE GUM, PACK	12
SNO-CAPS	8
CHIP A ROOS, PACKAGE	22
FRANKENBERRY STRAWBERRY-FLAVORED FROSTED CEREAL	41
MILK CHEW-ETS	12
PILLSBURY INSTANT CHOCOLATE MALT BREAKFAST	37

CRUNCHOLA PEANUT-BUTTER-AND-GRANOLA BARS	14
DIET SHASTA	22
BETTY CROCKER SNACKIN' CAKES	16
YODEL, INDIVIDUAL	16
STRAWBERRY TWIZZLERS	3
BRACH'S CANDY CORN	8
CARNATION CHOCOLATE CRUNCH BREAKFAST BAR	29
SNOWCREST NONPAREILS	4
CHERRYBERRY DIET DRINK	23
BURRY GAUCHOS, PACKAGE	19
SCOOTER PIE, INDIVIDUAL	17
NESTLÉ CHOCO-LITE	24
POST SUPER SUGAR CRISP	29
NABISCO CHUCKLES	7
PECAN SANDIES, PACKAGE	12
FUDGE MATE, INDIVIDUAL	8
RALSTON-PURINA DINKY DONUTS	29
YOO-HOO CHOCOLATE FLAVORED DRINK	44
SUZY Q, INDIVIDUAL	7
QUAKER CAP'N CRUNCH'S CRUNCHBERRIES	31
RICH' N CHIPS, PACKAGE	29
KELLOGG'S COCOA CRISPIES	34
GENERAL MILLS KIX CRISPY CORN PUFFS	29
SUNSHINE HYDROX COOKIES, ENTIRE PACKAGE CONSUMED	87

ETHNIC GUILT

Dear Occupant:

Thank you for opening this letter.

You probably have been asking yourself:

"How many bigots does it take to change a lightbulb?"

Well, the answer is simple. It takes *two*:

One to screw in the bulb...

...and one to make a filthy bigoted remark about it that your child may overhear and worry about until he has been permanently marked by the horror of the experience for the rest of his life!

Should rank bigotry be something that might scar your youngster's bright future?

Of course not. And that's why *we're* here. Who are we? We're the Anti-Bigotry League To Save Our Children's Peace of Mind (ABLTSOCPM). We hope that you will accept the enclosed small handmade Anti-Bigotry Doll (known to all as "Biggie") as our free gift to you, the Occupant, without any obligation whatsoever.

Just reflect for a moment, though, on how the scourge of bigotry might affect your small child's future—and how it could affect a youngster's mental health. Think

about Bill, Bob, and Buster Bigot out there, waiting to pounce on your tot and say unpardonable things that will send the child right to the psychiatrist's couch for the rest of his or her natural life.

Can your youngster afford to suffer such stigma? Can *you* afford the high fees charged by mental-health practitioners—fees that are expected to quadruple by the time your child reaches the optimal age of analysis? Wouldn't you much prefer to support our fine work, and prevent us from sending you more anti-bigotry dolls?

We are of the opinion that the only persons who would *not* contribute to our fine organization must be bigots themselves. That's why we automatically enroll all *non*-contributors in the "ABLTSOCPM Dishonor Roll," our famous bigotry listing. Remember, the Roll is entered annually in the Congressional Record, and distributed quarterly to some 209,450 employers, social agencies, and professional organizations across the land.

May the spirit of toleration bless the cheerful giver!

Warmly,
ABLTSOCPM

PARENT-BOOK GUILT

If I had *only* read Brazleton better, my son wouldn't have hit Tommy over the head with the Creative Playthings Building Block and made him start screaming. And if I don't buy that Fitzhugh Dodson book on fathering, I'll probably *never* know how to be a father. And Spock— well, he must have written one paragraph *somewhere* in there on sleep problems, but I must have slept through it. And, well, thank *you*, Dr. Lamaze, but what did I *not* read in your book that would explain why Evelyn still uses her puff-breathing techniques whenever she talks on the phone to my mother?

GUCCI GUILT

And, my God, they all had little alligators on their little Izod shirts, and Hermie had on the dirty "Best Little Whorehouse in Bayonne 1978" T-shirt that Grandpa gave him!

SALAMANDER GUILT

How is it possible for children to see five zillion stories about little doggies that are mistreated by their masters, and raccoons that are mistreated by people, and horses that are mistreated by their owners, and stories about salmon and dragonflies and little teeny mousies, all suffering horribly from mistreatment by insensitive people—how is it *possible* for them to see all that and still let the pet turtle they caught at the lake, the salamander they caught in the woods, the cute crayfish they caught by the river, die horrible deaths of starvation and neglect in their glass jars? And what am I supposed to do about it, other than rant and rave and feel sorry for the little beasts and feed the entire damn menagerie of pets myself?

JUNK-FOOD GUILT

And here's our tried-and-tested can't-fail recipe:

INGREDIENTS:

2 pkgs. Nacho Cheese Flavored Doritos
1 Filet-O-Fish Sandwich
2 slices Pizza Hut Thick 'n' Chewy Crust, medium pie
3 handfuls Cheese Nips
5 pieces Chicken McNuggets
2 holsters Roy Rogers fries
1 Burger King Happy Meal with Diet Sprite in Princess Leia glass
5 sips vanilla Arby shake
1 Hojo cola

INSTRUCTIONS: Blend above ingredients into child's diet, measuring (1) parent's unhappiness at doing same with (2) parent's inability to spend kitchen time preparing hearty, nutritious meals.

YIELD: Guilt.

LUNCH-BOX GUILT

MOMMIE: Ah, there's Fawn, our playmate here at the Little Purple Giraffe Day Care Center. What does little Fawnie have in her lunch box, hmmm?

FAWN: Kee.

MOMMIE: Kee? Ah, quiche, I see. Where'd you get that from, dear? Doggie bag from your dad's lunch? Oh, *Mom*, you say. Mom made it for you personally. Took her all yesterday afternoon, you say? Ah, but here's little Jennifer. What's she have in her Troy-Built lunch box, eh? What is that, dear?

JENNIFER: Buwwa bowwa.

MOMMIE: Huh? Let me see. Ah. *Bulgar Brownies.* Really? Mmm—so, well, nutritional. So marvelously healthy and, well, *Bulgarian,* don't you agree, Jennifer? Have a lovely snack. And what else is that, eh? You say *pavay*? A what? A pa–*vay*? Sweetie, shape your little bee-stung three-year-old lips so I can hear you better, honey. Try to talk a little more clearly, like my son, okay? So, how's your pavay? Oh, parfait, you're saying. Parfait! Oh, you say, a bee-cap parfait. And your dad just whipped it up in the Sanyo Food Processor this morning before he headed to the OR, did he?

(Aside, to son:)
Marvin, boy. Shhh! Marvin. Listen to me, kid. That bunch of peanut butter sticks I pack for you every single morning? The peanut butter smeared on white bread, cut into strips, and dumped into wax paper? You tell them all that it's Nutted Wheat Wedges, right? Nutted Wheat Wedges? Your mom ground the nuts and your dad grew the wheat. Marvin, got that? Marvin?

PIANO-LESSON GUILT

"Well, honey, I do kind of like those tiny little violins under their chins, and all of the kids holding their little bows at just the very same angle and all, but Roger was telling me that the Suzuki Method makes them into little *robots*, you know? That they can never ever attain, well, the *spontaneity* of a Heifetz if they learn the violin that way, is what Roger said.

"So maybe I should just take Tina over to Guitar World for lessons there? But Mr. Columbucci at Pianoland is so *fatherly*, I've always thought. And remember that boy he had who went to the Cliburn competition?

"But you know Tina really isn't that fabulously musical anyway, so I was wondering if maybe she'd be better off with Miss Montparnasse over there at Leotard Land? But the problem is that *Saturday morning* is also Tennis for Tots, at 10 A.M.

"The *real* problem is that Tina really doesn't want to take any lessons at all, and I really don't want to drive her all over the place, and my God, won't her future development always be stunted by denying her these essential learning experiences at this crucial age? And won't it be all my fault?"

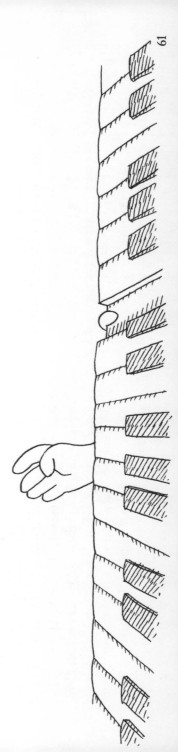

BIRTHDAY-PARTY GUILT

"Well, it's not exactly our *fault* that you were born in the summer and can't have a birthday party in your class at school, Howie."

•

"Gee, honey. Could you light that cake again? Somehow, well, the flashcube, it sort of stuck."

•

"Well, how could we know five different kids would give you the same *Star Wars* action figure, Howie?"

•

"Howie, Howie, don't worry about it! Just because you're the birthday boy doesn't mean that you have to win *all* the prizes in pin-the-tail-on-the-donkey. It's still a great party, isn't it? Howie?"

•

"Oh, you say that Morgan had plastic parachute kazoos as party favors at *his* party? Well, your birthday is still special. I mean, your name isn't Morgan, is it?"

•

"Howie, how were we to know the candles wouldn't light?"

•

"Why yes, Mrs. Biondolillo. There *are* holes in our living room couch. But it sure isn't keeping your son from having a great birthday party with our Howie. Want some more wine with your ice cream cake?"

•

"How could you doubt it, Howie! Of course your birthday party will be bigger next year. More presents, more kids, more noise."

•

"Hi, Mrs. Smithson. Here's my son, hope he has a wonderful time at your birthday party. Well, I can't stay, gotta run, be back in three hours, that's when it's over, right Mrs. Smithson? Oh? You hoped I could stay? You mean you think he'll cry if I'm not there?"

•

"Well, *so what* if Mr. Armando took all the kids up in the Goodyear Blimp for Victor's birthday party. Not every party can be totally special. Okay, okay, so Mrs. Anderson took all the kids to Scuba World and they had ice cream on a float in the diving tank. Honey, do *I* look like an aquanaut? Well, it's just great that Mr. Kroner is a pilot and Billy had his party in a 747 at the airport. But what's wrong with a nice little party in the Happy Room at Burgerland, huh?"

NUTRITION GUILT

"Well, dear, the best I can figure by reading the label on the Yodel here, it's got PARTIALLY HYDROGENATED VEGETABLE SHORTENING, THIAMINE MONONITRATE, DUTCH PROCESS COCOA (ALKALIZED), CAROB POWDER, SODIUM CASEINATE, MONO AND DIGLICERIDES, ISO-LATED SOY PROTEIN, SODIUM ALUMINUM PHOSPHATE WITH ALUMINUM SULFATE, CALCIUM CASEINATE, SORBI-TAN MONOSTEARATE AND POLYSORBATE 60, VANILLIN (ARTIFICIAL FLAVOR), AND SODIUM PROPIONATE.

"I don't think we'll feel too awful if he has just one of these in his lunch box today, do you, honey?"

GRANDPARENT GUILT

I can't stand it! The *kids* want to see more of Grandpa and Grandma—and *Grandpa and Grandma* want to see more of the kids. The only one who doesn't want to see Grandpa and Grandma so much is *me*, and that's because I'm the one who happened to grow *up* with them.

MATH-AND-SCIENCE GUILT

THE PROBLEM: Worried parent (P) and confused child (C) accelerate toward each other across kitchen table (T). Equidistant from parent (P) and child (C) upon surface of table (T) are a mathematics textbook (T_1) and a science textbook (T_2).

The confusion of child (C) accelerates at steady rate (R+r+r+r) as child (C) asks, "But Dad, how am I ever going to *do* this stuff?" Parent (P) attempts to decelerate confusion at a steady rate (R-r-r-r) as he replies cheerily, "Well, son, just how tough could this little Calculus Carnival project be, eh?"

Parent (P) proceeds to help child (C). Parent (P) becomes more and more involved (t^2) in project as time (t) passes. However, child (C) starts doodling, staring off into space, humming, and looking yearningly toward the television listings.

QUESTION: At exactly what point will parent (P) and child (C) achieve a head-on collision across kitchen table (T)? Will child (C) be sent directly to bed (B)?

TRAIN-SET GUILT

"When you change the switches on the tracks that way, Howie, the locomotives are going to crash. Here, look, let me show you. You put *this* track length here, see, next to the Anthracite Coal Mine and the Lumberjack Village, and throw this switch here near the Old Trestle Bridge. Right? Wait, Howie! I have to wire the signals! Here, give me those controls. Now, let me just put the roundhouse at the other end of the switchyard.

"Howie? What do you mean you want to watch TV? What do you mean I won't let you play with your new train set?"

EXERCISE GUILT

"Allie, Daddy will be gone jogging for just a little while, just an hour and a half or so, and then he'll be right back and we can start putting together that 13,000-piece H.M.S. *Bounty* jigsaw puzzle. No, honey, I really can't start on it now. I've just gotta get outside! But I'll be *right back.*"

•

"Now look, hon. Mom and I will be back from our walk before you can say, 'Time for bed!'"

•

"Surely Daddy can just swim out to the lifeguard buoy *once* while you do the castle walls yourself for a minute, right? Well, why on earth *can't* you wreck the moat while I'm away?"

•

"No, Tommie, I told you never to ask me questions while I'm working out on the Nautilus. It ruins my concentration. Oh. You brought me some water. Well, I mean, thanks, big guy."

•

"I'd just love to take apart and put back together your Big Honcho Play Copter, Terr. But see, Mom and I, we're just gonna play a couple more sets. You know, we just adore this game."

•

"Rebecca, of course you can come riding with Mom on your tricycle! But see, Mom just has this incredibly tremendous need right this minute to take the ten-speed for a fast spin out to the Point and back. And see, I don't think you can keep up, hon."

SUNDAY-NIGHT GUILT

"How *could* we have forgotten Meteor Identification Day at the museum?"

"I'm just sorry we all missed seeing *The Shaggy Dog from Outer Space* together. You know, it could have been a really *nice* time."

•

"Oh, God! I was going to spend the entire morning making General Custer's cavalry flag with the boys. And now look at the time."

•

"You know, we were going to braid the girls' hair tonight, and now it's their bedtime."

•

"What I *wanted* to do was take the kids over to the state fair at Loganport. I'd have loved it, they'd have loved it, you'd have loved it. And what we *did* was Midge's anniversary party, and fix the water heater, for God's sake."

•

"Could I really have forgotten to buy Phillie a new composition book? And where do I get one Monday morning before school?"

•

"And where did the time go, anyway?"

•

"Next weekend, it's gonna be *different*."

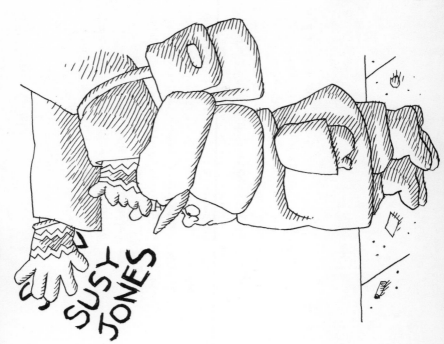

ON-THE-STREET-WHERE-YOU-LIVE GUILT

CITY GUILT

The urban parent's case for city guilt:

My kids don't have the *freedom* and the *intimate association with nature* that I did as a kid. Farm children would be out sugaring this very second. I have stolen something sacred from their childhood!

City kids are exposed to *ideas, dangers, and dirty words* at too young an age, and are being robbed of their very right to be children.

Air pollution, noise pollution, and water pollution will make them into stunted gnomes, and they won't be able to get into Stanford then.

The competitive environment will make them too *smart and challenging*, and turn them into *teen-age werewolves* who hate their mom and dad.

It would all be so different if only they were in the suburbs or the country. And it's my fault!

SUBURBAN GUILT

The split-level parent's case for suburban guilt:

My kids are absolute marshmallows in this dud of a community. They are getting no intellectual or cultural stimulation. Their brains are turning to lox.

It's too safe and idyllic here! These kids are developing no street smarts whatsoever and will be totally unable to compete with city kids for the rest of their lives.

My kids have no independence whatsoever, they have to be driven *everywhere*, they never see poverty or want, and they are developing the *wrong values*.

This town encourages children to *be* children until they're in college. All they aspire to be is mindless high school lummoxes out for a good time, selfish kids with no sense of adult responsibility whatsoever!

It would be so different if only they lived in the city.

And it's my fault!

COUNTRY GUILT

The rural parent's case for country guilt:

My kids are so isolated and lonely, they'll only be fit to be fur trappers when they grow up.

So what if the kids are raising 4-H heifers and reading the book of the woods? The schools out here will never give my kids the preparation those fancy city and suburban schools do.

There's too much nature here! The kids will never be able to survive in a city. And my kids are out so much in the sun, swimming and fishing and being in the outdoors, they'll *never* want to crack a book or knuckle down to working when they grow up.

There just aren't enough playmates for them in this whole county! My kids are around me so much of the time in the winter that they have no other role models, and they'll grow up to be just as crazy as I am!

We're so old-fashioned out here. How will my kids ever compete with those city kids?

It would be so different if only they lived in the city or the suburbs. And it's all my fault!

PEER-GROUP GUILT

"I mean, just how are you going to get your Rhodes Scholarship in the first place, hanging out with friends like Doo-Wah, Switch, and Wheelie?

"Son, I guess what I'm saying is I think your friend Danny is going *right* to reform school. And *Herbie*— well, the collection of truck-tire liners he's been putting together is a nice hobby and all, but is it going to get him to college? And that girl Doreen you all hang around with, I mean it's nice that she likes to visit old graveyards, but I sometimes wonder whether her porch lights are really *on*, you know?

"Oh, it's *my* fault? For moving into this neighborhood in the first place when you could have stayed with your friends in the city? Well, excuse me, but aren't there *any* other kids you could hang around with?"

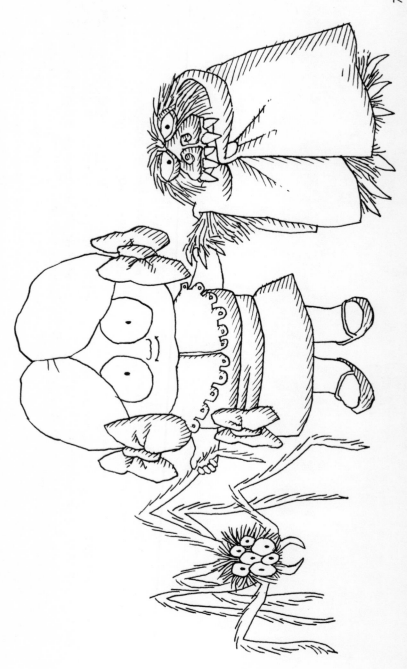

DINNER-TABLE CONVERSATION GUILT

Well, what I want to know is, if Joseph P. Kennedy could lead all his children in dinner discussions of Back Bay politics and the economy and international relations, and if those kids could go on to be presidents and senators and world leaders, then what is wrong with this father?

As near as I can tell, we have just spent the last ten minutes talking about Lisa's saddle shoes. Oh, yes, Georgie also expressed his forthright opinion on the beef stew, which he found not quite suited to his taste. I believe Georgie was also less than enthusiastic about the green beans. The previous topic of conversation was, if I have it right, the Tooth Fairy. What was the gist? Oh, yes—that the rumor among the children of this family was that the Tooth Fairy is going to be giving two dollars to lucky small fry this year. I believe I commented that any child who believes *that* is probably foolish enough to believe in the Tooth Fairy! That was, I believe, when Mother kicked me under the table. Well, they never kicked Joseph P. Kennedy under the table, I can tell you that!

RELIGION GUILT

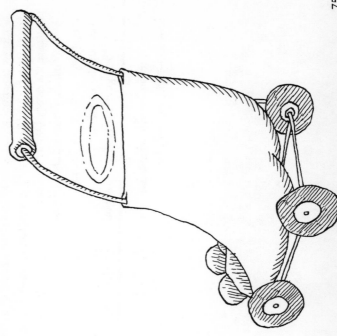

Well, we always *intended* to go to church, you know? I don't know exactly why it is we don't go. Everything is so hectic with the jobs and the kids, you know. And so we just sort of don't go to church. Well, really, we don't have the time, you know, first of all. We're usually out at the country house on Sundays. And the kids get sort of bored with the whole thing, and we're both so tired after working all week and then doing errands on Saturday, that, well, we just sort of assume a horizontal position on Sunday. And you know, well, the TV is a lot better on Sunday morning than it ever used to be, I'll tell you that! And somehow I never liked the new pastor after old Reverend Norcross moved to that parish in Sarasota.

The thing is, though, whenever we're really in trouble, we say to ourselves, "God help me *out*." We know how to pray. And we believe.

But the way we're raising these kids, well, they'll never say that to themselves. Ever. They've hardly been inside a *church*, for God's sake. And they'll never say "For God's sake" to themselves, either! I didn't much like going to church when I was a kid, but what I'm wondering is, well, is our way of raising them any better?

TEACHER GUILT

"Well, the basic problem is they're going to put him in Miss Blunderman's class next year.

"I know, dear, I know. Look, I told the principal that our son's emotional growth would be stunted! I said his academic potential would suffer! I said he was being torn from all his friends! I even said I'd volunteer again to organize the Arbor Day Tree Picnic!

"Well, they said no. They said no! Honey, I did *everything* I could to get Tommy into Mrs. Sunshine's class, and they said no.

"So I guess we have no choice but to settle for Miss Blunderman.

"I mean, despite what we've heard about her, just how bad could she really be?"

SINGLE-PARENT GUILT

Dear Diary,

Today, Annie's third-grade teacher tried to be *very* helpful. She said, "Annie, you don't have to make Father's Day presents with us because you come from a broken home." How do I get across the idea to Annie that our house doesn't need fixing?

Dear Diary,

Well, today the school principal invited *all* the kids to the annual "Breakfast with Dad" get-together. Well, their dad might just make it if he drove 2,250 miles.

Dear Diary,

Well, nice going, Mom. Today we delivered the plywood stable that Mom and her kids made all weekend for the Christmas pageant. A nice job of carpentry. And guess what note Mom got back from the music teacher? "Thank you, Mr. Jones."

Dear Diary,

You just hang in there, Mrs. Jones.

VIOLENT-SOCIETY GUILT

The kind of world I would like to live in is a world:

(A) where my children will not find out about the robbery next door.

(B) where my children will *not* hear of the mugging down the block.

(C) where TV newscasters will not interrupt 8 P.M. children's specials with bulletins about news of more Atlanta murders coming up at 11 o'clock.

(D) where my children will not accidentally hear about stickups, shootings, and presidential assassinations on the radio before I can change the station.

(E) where they won't see gory pictures in newspapers and magazines that have been left around by mistake.

(F) where I won't worry about what the knowledge of all this violence is doing to my children.

I know where that world is. It's in a theme park. It's called Fantasyland.

TOY GUILT

"Davie, frankly, your mom and me, we feel you just have *too many* toys. You never play with them. We think you're getting spoiled, and, well, I think that's our fault. I mean, you don't even know what to *do* with all the toys in this room.

"What's that, Davie? You don't have what? You don't have an Astro Phaser 3000 Play Pak? Every other kid in your class has one? It's *our fault* that none of the other kids invite you to their house? My God, Davie, why didn't you tell me about this before? We'll get one immediately!"

SCHOOL GUILT

PUBLIC-SCHOOL GUILT

So I went to the principal. I said, "This teacher thinks that subtraction is a submarine housing development, that division is something you see with, and she wouldn't know a part of speech from the part she sits down with." And I said that the teacher won't give homework because she couldn't be bothered to check it, and they don't seem to teach spelling or writing or grammar anymore, so what do they *do* all day in class?

And the principal says, "They try to play traffic cop for the forty kids in the room, that's what, and if you don't like it, take your little darling over to St. Matilda's of the Golden Coffers and see how your kid likes that."

And I said I'd just *love* to do that, except who can afford private school? But my God I have a smart kid there and the public schools aren't teaching her a *single thing* and I feel so awful about it! It's a baby-sitting service, that's all, and this is the only education my daughter is ever going to get, and she's losing her big chance, and I can't afford private school, and I'm failing her, and someday will she forgive me?

PRIVATE-SCHOOL GUILT

I couldn't stop torturing myself. I thought, *Mr. Big Deal,* what would Miss FitzGerald think? Or Mr. Zakon? What would *he* think, the best science teacher who ever lived? You're beyond P.S. 185 now. *You* have to send your kid to some private school for as much money this year as your entire undergraduate college tuition?

Well, Mr. Big Deal, you turned out pretty well, didn't you, Mr. Junior High School 259? But the public schools aren't good enough for *your* kids? You want them to become spoiled little rich kids, like the ones you hated when you were in public school? Well, you make your bed and you lie in it, Mr. Smartie. If you don't want to give your kids the chance to make their own way, to compete with other normal kids, to fend for themselves in a public school and learn the value of life and laughter and making it on their own with good solid kids from striving families, *instead of tycoons' kids who only want to deal dope,* then you deserve what you get! Class 6-1 in P.S. 185 would be pretty ashamed of you right now, I can tell you!

VERI I EM BADLIE EDUKATED

VACATION GUILT

Q: What is Vacation Guilt, Doctor?

A: Vacation Guilt is an extremely common parental ailment. Attacks are frequently brought on during the 54-Ramada-Inn tour of Great Cavern Country.

Q: What are its symptoms, Doctor?

A: The symptoms are manifested in parents' intense feelings of guilt at the sight of bored, cranky children who are mooning and moping around throughout the vacation. Often the youngsters have scarcely enough energy to put on their socks. They whine during long automobile trips. They set fire to the AAA Tour Guide in the back seat with a magnifying glass.

Q: But why do parents feel guilty about this behavior?

A: Because they have taken the children on a trip that they, the *parents*, enjoy. The adults feel guilty that they have snatched their children from their friends and from their usual activities.

Q: Then the guilt can be cured if the parents take their children to a lake, a seaside resort, or vacation community, Where the children can make friends and not be bored?

A: Unfortunately, no.

Q: Why, doctor?

A: Then the parents will still have guilty feelings—that they never do anything for their *own* vacation enjoyment. The parents will feel increasingly bored, their tensions will erupt in squabbles, they will fight about it for much of the summer, they will snap at the kids and feel even *more* guilty for doing so. And then they will vow, *next summer*, to go on a 54-Ramada-Inn tour of Shaved Ice Caves and the Crystal Cavern Country. Is that completely clear?

Thank you, doctor.

BEDTIME GUILT

7:52 P.M.: *"Ten minutes till bedtime!"*

8:03 P.M.: *"Okay, honey, that's really it, now, bedtime."*

8:05 P.M.: *"Okay, that's really really it."*

8:09 P.M.: *"Aren't you in bed yet?"*

8:11 P.M.: *"What do you mean, where did I put your blue Magic Marker? You're not using Magic Markers— you're getting to bed."*

8:12 P.M.: *"I don't care what you're making! You get ready for bed, young lady."*

8:14 P.M.: *"Tears won't help a bit. Now get in those jammies and brush those teeth, you hear?"*

8:17 P.M.: *"No, I don't want to hear what you were using the Magic Marker for out on the dining room table. Get to bed."*

8:32 P.M.: *"That's better. Now that you're in bed, can I read you a story? Maybe you'll stop crying then?"*

8:33 P.M.: *"You don't ever want a story? And you'll hate me for the rest of my life? Well, I was just trying to get you to bed, for God's sake. Good-night, honey. I'm going out to clean up the dining room."*

8:37 P.M.: *"Hey! Honey! Were you making this beautiful Valentine's Day card for your old dad? Is that what you were making? Honey?"*

8:38 P.M.: *"Baby, you're asleep already?"*

84

CRAFTS GUILT

See, in this family, it's a major feat of creative artistry just to get everyone's socks on in the morning. But then there are families like the Smithsons. They do *crafts* with their children. Here is what we heard ourselves saying, the last time we visited:

"Gee, I'd never have *thought* you could teach a three-year-old to tie-dye her whole wardrobe! You're such a creative mother!"

"My, and you've macramed all your diapers and wouldn't *dream* of using Pampers! You folks are *just so talented!*"

"You and the kids made that whole huge quilt entirely on a pot-holder weaver? Didn't the little cloth-covered rubber bands shoot all over the kitchen, the way they do whenever I try to use them?"

"Pipe-cleaner people on the Christmas tree, too! And you all made them together in front of the fireplace! Now why didn't *our* family think of that!"

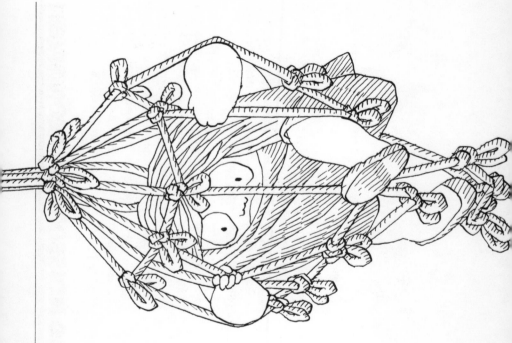

MEANINGFUL-DISCUSSION GUILT

Well, I was going to spend all morning with Geoffie just answering all his many questions about the dirty words he must be hearing in school, you know? Really answer every question, nothing is out of bounds for good old Dad to explain, but then I had to fix the lawn sprinkler and Geoffie got invited over to Mac's playhouse and then, well, it was dinner time, so we just didn't get around to it, is the problem.

And I wanted to tell Tobie all about what she should do on the street—say, if a strange man offers her a Fudgsicle, and, you know, tell her without *scaring* her and all, but yet make her aware of all the dangers even though she says she knows everything, you know? But then I had to go over to Lumber World, and Tobie's friends were around later and I didn't want to embarrass her, and I just never got to it, but gee, I feel really bad that I didn't.

DIVORCE GUILT

It's really stupid, you know? But somehow I can't get it out of my head. I keep daydreaming that Ozzie Nelson would never have *married* someone he'd someday get divorced from. Or if he *bad*, well, they'd have worked it out. Though I guess I couldn't work it out. And Ozzie would never have blamed himself the way I keep doing. And Dave and Ricky, well, they would never have blamed *themselves* for the whole thing, felt it had been their fault,

like my kids do. And the Nelson kids would never have been as wild in school this year, divorce or no divorce. And Ozzie, well, he wouldn't have felt so uptight bringing his new girlfriends home. Or if he had, the Nelson kids wouldn't have been so unpleasant about it. And Ozzie would never have felt so guilty about the whole mess. Not Robert Young either...or Fred MacMurray.

Thank God Desi and Lucy know how I feel.

VISITING-RIGHTS GUILT

9:00 A.M.: Pick up Sandy.

9:33 A.M.: Buy Sandy package of Bubblicious gum.

10:00 A.M.: Arrive at *Peter and the Wolf* recital.

11:00 A.M.: Buy Sandy Mello-Roll vanilla ice cream cone.

11:15 A.M.: Arrive at Children's Zoo.

11:16 A.M.: Buy Sandy Cracker Jacks.

12:00 noon: Buy Sandy hot dog and Jujubes.

12:15 P.M.: Buy Sandy balloon.

12:30 P.M.: Buy Sandy vanilla ice cream sandwich.

1:00 P.M.: Arrive at natural history museum "Kids' Kraft-In."

1:02 P.M.: Buy Sandy key chain at museum shop.

2:00 P.M.: Buy Sandy chocolate milk in museum cafeteria.

2:30 P.M.: Leave natural history museum.

2:31 P.M.: Buy Sandy pretzel from pretzel man.

2:55 P.M.: Arrive at movie theater for *Fantasia* showing.

2:57 P.M.: Buy Sandy small Sprite and popcorn.

3:42 P.M.: Buy Sandy package of Junior Mints.

4:50 P.M.: Leave movie theater.

4:54 P.M.: Buy Sandy Wonder Woman comic book.

5:10 P.M.: Arrive at Burgerland.

5:14 P.M.: Buy Sandy Burgerland Jolly Meal with Jolly Shake in a Jolly Glass.

6:12 P.M.: Deliver Sandy to her mother.

6:17 P.M.: Buy self drink.

SLEEPOVER GUILT

"Honey, why are you crying?"

"Dunno."

"Look now, you were sleeping over at Sharon's, you're gone for two whole days, and the first thing you do is burst into tears when you see me! Why?"

"Dunno Mom."

"My God, what'd they do to you over there? Wait a minute—did Sharon's big brother hang you out the window by your pigtails again like he did last time? Well?"

"No, Mom."

"My God, did they make you eat those horrible soda-bread toaster pizzas again?"

"No, Mom."

"Well, what then? Did they force you to watch slides of their trip to Great Husky Vacationland again?"

"No, Mom."

"Honey! Those idiots didn't dare force you to sleep with the Labrador retriever pups again? Did they? Is that what they did?"

"No, Mom."

"Well, for God's sake! What happened? What did they do?"

"Oh, I dunno."

"You answer me!"

"Well, first we went out to dinner on their friend's yacht out at Safe Harbor. Their friend, he was visiting, he's from Bermuda and he travels all the time on his yacht and we all had dinner there. And, Mom? He hired a real string quartet to play music while we ate. And then afterwards, we all sailed over to Hunter's Island. You know what? They were filming this movie there, you know? And so we got to go on as extras. And there was this last scene with Bo Derek, see, she kisses Robert Redford, and Sharon actually got to talk to him afterwards, Mom. Although I only got his autograph. Anyway, it was real exciting. And then that family friend from Bermuda, he gave us all ice cream back on his yacht, and all of us went to sleep on board and woke up early the next morning and went swimming, and then spent the day fishing and sailing, Mom. And when Sharon and I left the boat, well, he gave us each a long-stemmed rose, Mom. To keep! And then I came home and when I saw you, Mom, I just started to cry, I don't know why, Mom."

"Oh."

"But it had nothing to do with you, Mom. I mean, I was really glad to see you again. Honest I was."

AUTOMOBILE GUILT

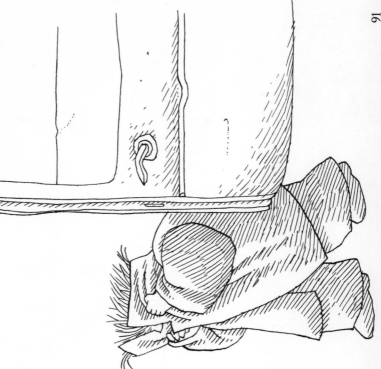

"Oh, I see. Freddie is absolutely the neatest kid in the class because his father has a black Trans-Am? Chopped and channeled? Oh, and Billy's a nerd because his mother drives him around in a brown Pacer. I see. And Nickie is a winner because his family drops him off in a Dodge TransVan with bubble windows? I get it. I get it. And Tony is God because his cousin once parked a Maserati in his driveway?

"So. What does that make us, huh?

"Oh, yeah?

"Well, I'll stack up a 1973 Plymouth Valiant against any car anytime anywhere! Oh, you're embarrassed learning to drive in a brown Valiant with a dirty white vinyl roof? Well, I can't *afford* a $30,000 Mercedes, okay? And do those cars have the 225 Valiant big six? You can't even buy that anymore! Well, if I'm not ashamed of it, then why are you ashamed of it?"

FAMILY-SIZE GUILT

LARGE-FAMILY GUILT

"Look, if five of us go to the movie, well, that's twenty bucks right there, then we just even *pass by* the drive-through window at McDonald's and it's another fifteen bucks at least, twenty if we get the apple pies in a wrapper, and I thought we were saving for college, though just try to save anything when you get four kids two new pairs of jeans every time we go to the mall, just try it!

"You know, it's great fun to have a large family, and I wouldn't do it over again any other way. But sometimes I don't feel too great about it, you know? If we had only one of you, we could afford to send you to good schools and buy you lots of good things and not have to scrimp and save and constantly try to make ends meet!

"But then, if we had only one of you, well, just *who* would clean out the garbage, which is exactly what the four of you lunkheads are going to do this minute or I am going to know exactly why, I can tell you!"

ONLY-CHILD GUILT

I'm so glad the research is clear about the whole thing. An only child is blessed, that's all there is to it. The only child is a high achiever. He generally does well throughout life. There is absolutely no evidence that the only child suffers from being an only child—emotionally, developmentally, or cognitively. And now there are playgroups, child cooperatives, nursery schools, and day-care centers, so an only child doesn't have to be smothered or spoiled by her parents.

So why does every *grown-up* only child I know have a minimum of two kids, huh? You think they know something we don't? Well, I think they do! They know you don't have a real family unless two kids are giggling in the back of the station wagon!

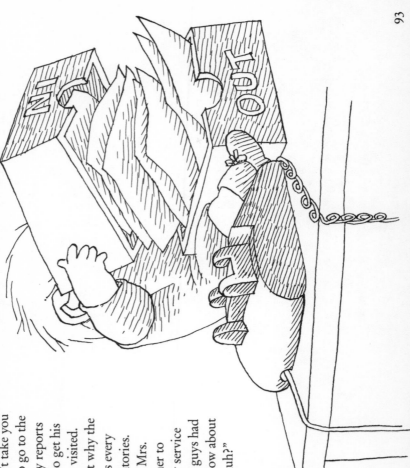

DON'T-TAKE-'EM-TO-THE-OFFICE-ENOUGH GUILT

"Yes, I guess I *am* feeling guilty that I don't take you guys to the office more. I know you kids *love* to go to the office! But it's just that we're doing the quarterly reports now, see, and Mr. Grolsch still hasn't been able to get his calculator working again from the last time you visited. And Mrs. Katcherarian? She still can't figure out why the computer printout machine runs rocket pictures every once in a while in the middle of the flange inventories. Maybe you guys *did* something to it, huh? And Mrs. Kuchel is still a bit ticked off at me for leaving her to watch you guys while I went on that emergency service call. You remember how when I came back you guys had tied her all up with the adding machine tape? How about we go in some Saturday when nobody's there, huh?"

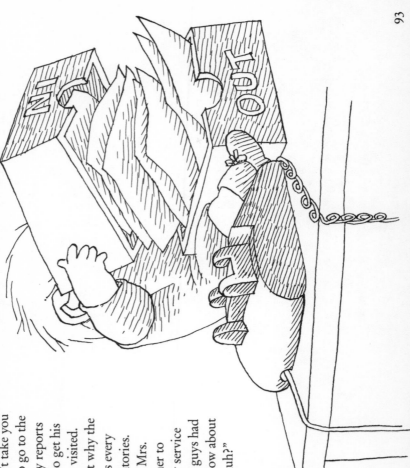

HAND-ME-DOWN GUILT

"Well, it was good enough for your brother, wasn't it?"

"So, if it was good enough for your big sister, what's wrong with *you?*"

•

"Just pull on the neck a little, hon. Then it'll fit."

"The nice thing about those shoes is that your brother broke them all in for you."

"Not every child can go through life without patches on all his pants."

•

"Honey, you *want* a loose fit with that kind of coat."

"So what if it's an old *Empire Strikes Back* shirt and not a *Revenge of the Jedi* shirt? Doesn't make any difference to *me.*"

•

"Oh, you'll grow into those pants in no time."

•

"Well, if you look up to your brother so much, why do you hate his gloves so much?"

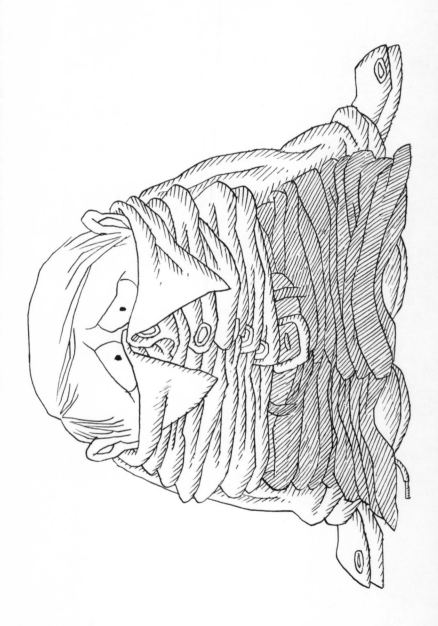

WHAT-DOES-YOUR-DADDY-DO GUILT

"Class, I just don't know that there's a luckier bunch of fourth graders anywhere! This year, you've already had quite a wonderful group of parents telling you about their occupations. There was Mr. Throckmorton, Tommy's dad, who came to talk about being a bond lawyer. And then there was Tina's dad, Dr. Gregory, who told us all about being a gastroenterologist. And Horace's father, Mr. Simon, explained what it was like to run a bank, where everyone puts their money!

"Well, then. I'm very pleased that Hermie's father, Mr. Dombrowsky, is with us today. He'll be telling us what it's like to be a bartender. So let's give him a big hand, shall we?"

WORK-A-DADDY GUILT

"Davie? See, the distributor's meeting, it lasted right through lunch, so I couldn't see you in the play. No, I was just stuck there in that room. But look at this! I got it for you in Pick 'n' Pay on the way home! And looky here! Have you ever seen an actual Management by Objective Flow Chart inventory form? You haven't? Well *look* what I've got here for *you*."

FAMILY-FUN GUILT

"What do you mean this isn't fun? You're bored, are you? In the largest and oldest continuously run state fair in the Pacific Northwest? You're not having *fun*? Donnie is tired of going on rides, is he? Oh, you wish you were back home watching television?

"Oh, don't *you* start in, Annie! You want your *other* pacifier, do you? The one you left on the dashboard when we closed up the car in the sun, the one that's now 2000 degrees and melting down on the floor mats? Well, I'm not going back to that parking lot! What kind of fun is that for me?

"Oh, is that right, Donnie! You stored the cotton candy for keeps in my purse! *What is wrong with this family?* What is wrong with *me?* We are never ever all together, and today we finally are, and I just want us to have a little *family fun*, like every other family can, and we never seem to be able to do it! What is wrong with us? Why can't we be like normal human American families and have fun like they do?"

SUMMER-CAMP GUILT

Dear Mom,

Things are all goine prety well here now that Mr. Famigucci finally fixed the carbaraytor. He couldn't fix the carbaraytor for two days which is why he couldn't go into town, ha ha. But, well, he's gone into town now so everything is ok.

I'ts ok because in town he got the super glue to fix the pot. The pot was leakine all the time, mom, all over the floor and everything, and now that Mr. Famigucci brought the super glue to fix the pot it hasn't been leakine at all.

This is good, mom, because it means that we only have to empty the pot every 45 minutes about. That's better than the pot leakine on the floor all the time like it was. So now the cabin is pretty dry as long as we

remember to empty the pot, ha ha.

It's been rainine for eight days now mom, and we sure are glad Mr. Famigucci fixed the pot, because otherwise the leak in the roof would make us wetter and much more miserable than all of us are now. Mr. Famigucci can't fix the roof until it stops rainine, if it ever does.

Anyway mom I hope you have a nice vacation away from us noisy kids, ha ha. But me and Pammie are thinkine about you all the time and how dry it is in our basement and our kitchen and everything.

Hope you miss me like I miss you,

Debbie

PS.: Sorry for the wet spots on this letter, ha ha.

COLLEGE-TRACKING GUILT

Three reasons why Vannie, age two, won't get into Stanford:

(1) The Baby Blue Elephant Day Space has lost *every single one* of its little Fisher-Price people that fit into the Fisher-Price airport and the firehouse and the fire trucks and the police cars....

(2) In the two-year-old room? There is not a single page in the *Pat the Bunny* book that has one single thing left in it to pat or scratch or touch.

(3) And the Math Magnets? Did you notice how they got all bent when Jacob put them in the Tonka Big Boy Automobile Crusher?

So: You consider these facts about her education thus far and you actually think that somehow our Vannie is going to get into Stanford? Oh, you do? Well, that's not what I think! I think we've already doomed her to Hot-Comb Repair School!

TELEVISION GUILT

"Well, Doctor, what I wonder is, if I've been having a nervous breakdown *all Saturday morning* and the twins won't even let me make myself a cup of coffee, is it so *completely* awful if they watch *Barbapapa* at 6 A.M., *Magilla Gorilla* at 6:30, *Davey and Goliath* at 7, *Rainbow Patch* at 7:30, *The Flintstones* at 8, *Smurfs* at 8:30, *Scooby Doo* at 9, *Kid Super Power* at 9:30, *Spider-Man* at 10:30, *Space Stars* at 11, *Trollkins* at noon, *Bullwinkle* at 12:30, *Our Gang* at 1:00, followed by *Godzilla?* "Doctor?"

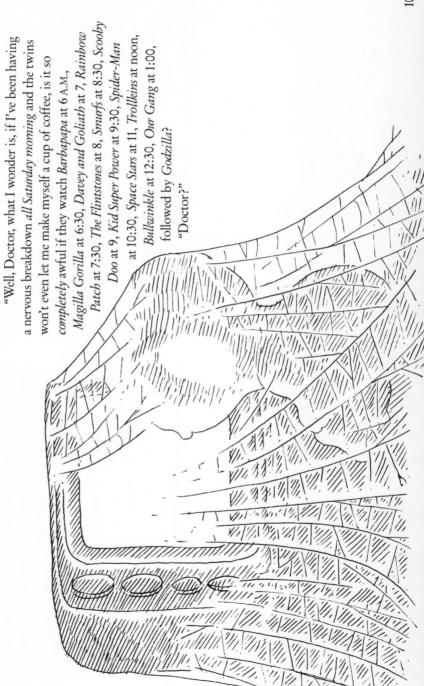

LITTLE-LEAGUE GUILT

(STRIKE ONE.) "Honey, I know you play better than most of the boys on the team, but Coach Kong feels that girls shouldn't play ice hockey, and I've talked and talked to him, but the guy *will not budge*. It's his own league, after all! Couldn't you go out for the Soccerettes? What's so great about the Hockey Hulks anyhow?"

(STRIKE TWO.) "All I said was that you could've stolen home! I did *not* say that you were worse than every other Little Legioner. Well, that's news to me! You hate baseball and you always wanted to build models in the basement? Well, why didn't you ever say so? No, you *didn't* tell me. Would I ever push you to excel at a sport when you hate the very thought of it?"

(STRIKE THREE.) "Look, Georgie, city kids can play ball just like any kids *anywhere!* What's so terrible about Mr. Broncoskco picking you guys up after school in his school bus and taking all of you guys out to Kennedy Point to play ball? You know, suburban kids don't have any benefit of personal instruction from a former Triple B Major leaguer like Mr. Broncoskco!"

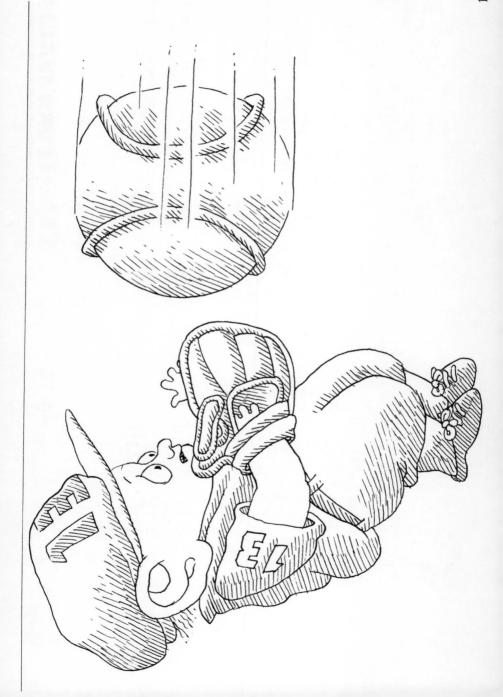

103

FUTURE GUILT

WASHINGTON, D.C. (*Combined Services*)—What will college students in the year 2000 be able to look forward to? "Well, they certainly won't be living in the comforting world of their parents," said Dudgeon P. Gipp, director of the Future Watch Institute here in northwest Washington.

Mr. Gipp explained that overpopulation and declining resources will strain the nation's educational fabric to the limit in the year 2000. "Much of the world, including the United States, may be beset by nuclear conflict, worldwide economic depression, famine, and consumer-good scarcity," he said. "And students will be competing harder for fewer spaces in the best colleges."

However, good colleges will always survive, he said. The problem for parents may be paying for them, though: "Inflation will make the cost of college tuition $129,000 a year by the date 2000," said Mr. Gipp.

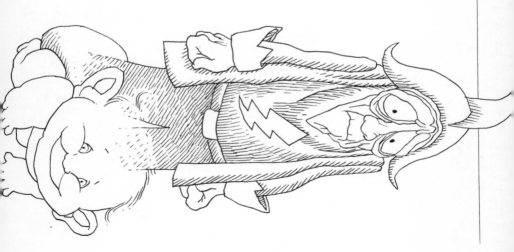

CHILDLESS GUILT

This is the regret that you never fulfilled yourself, never took the risk and braved the terror of raising children. At least that's one guilt you'll *never* be feeling.

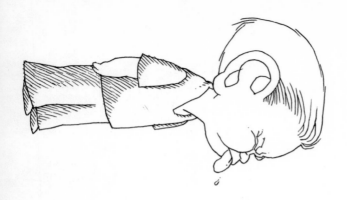

GLENN COLLINS is a reporter for *The New York Times*, where he writes about families, children, and behavior. He lives in Manhattan with his wife, Sarah, and their children, Brian and Alex. His most impressive achievement in parental guilt, "Total Number of Airport Toys Bought on Out-of-Town Trips," is not under active consideration by the *Guinness Book of World Records*.

GAHAN WILSON was a good boy. He descended from P.T. Barnum and William Jennings Bryan and tried very hard not to make his parents feel guilty, but failed, of course. He hopes his being a boy magician and his cartoons in *The New Yorker* and *Playboy*, his regular commentaries on National Public Radio, and his numerous book collections have cheered them up at least a little.